Countries Around the World

New Zealand

Mary Colson

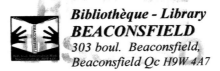
Heinemann Library
Chicago, Illinois

www.capstonepub.com
Visit our website to find out more information about Heinemann-Raintree books.

To order:
☎ Phone 800-747-4992
⌨ Visit www.capstonepub.com to browse our catalog and order online.

Edited by Catherine Veitch and Charlotte Guillain
Designed by Steve Mead
Original illustrations © Capstone Global Library Ltd 2012
Illustrated by Oxford Designers & Illustrators
Picture research by Hannah Taylor
Originated by Capstone Global Library Ltd
Printed in the United States of America in Eau Claire, Wisconsin.
052013   007421RP

15 14 13
10 9 8 7 6 5 4 3

Library of Congress Cataloging-in-Publication Data
Colson, Mary.
  New Zealand / Mary Colson.
    p. cm.—(Countries around the world)
  Includes bibliographical references and index.
  ISBN 978-1-4329-6106-0 (hb)—ISBN 978-1-4329-6132-9 (pb) 1.
New Zealand—Juvenile literature. I. Title.
  DU408.C65 2012
  993—dc22
                        2011015804

Acknowledgments
We would like to thank the following for permission to reproduce photographs: Alamy Images pp. 21 (© Suzanne Long), 27 (© Greg Balfour Evans), 9 (© John Elk III); Alexander Turnbull Library, Wellington, New Zealand p. 7; Bridgeman Art Library p. 8 (Alexander Turnbull Library, Wellington, New Zealand); Getty Images pp. 6 (Bridgeman Art Library), 29 (WireImage), 31 (Jeff J Mitchell); istockphoto p. 15 (© Mykhaylo); Photolibrary pp. 18 (OSF/Robin Bush), 24 (age fotostock/David Wall), 28 (LOOK-foto/travelstock44), 30 (Dallas and John Heaton), 38 (Imagebroker/FB-Fischer); Rex Features pp. 34 (Stephen Barker), 35 (Newspix/Craig Greenhill); Shutterstock pp. 5 (© Woody Ang), 11 (© Gr8), 13 (© Chester Tugwell), 14 (© Dennis Albert Richardson), 17 (© Matthew Fry), 19 (© KIS), 20 (© Jiri Foltyn), 22 (© Sam DCruz), 25 (© B.S.Karan), 33 (© Robyn Mackenzie).

Cover photograph of a Māori totem reproduced with permission of Photolibrary (Tips Italia/Andrea Pistolesi).

Every effort has been made to contact copyright holders of material reproduced in this book. Any omissions will be rectified in subsequent printings if notice is given to the publisher.

The author would like to thank Tim Dryden and Nathan Penny for their invaluable assistance in the preparation of this book. The publisher would also like to thank Harshan Kumarasingham for his valuable assistance in the preparation of this book.

Disclaimer
All the Internet addresses (URLs) given in this book were valid at the time of going to press. However, due to the dynamic nature of the Internet, some addresses may have changed, or sites may have changed or ceased to exist since publication. While the author and publisher regret any inconvenience this may cause readers, no responsibility for any such changes can be accepted by either the author or the publisher.

Contents

Some words in the book are in bold, **like this**. You can find out what they mean by looking in the glossary.

Introducing New Zealand

What do you think of when you picture New Zealand? Do you picture birds that cannot fly, or kiwi fruit? Do you think of people playing dangerous sports? Or maybe you imagine amazing scenery?

Located in the remote South Pacific Ocean, New Zealand is a land of mighty mountains, rushing rivers, spectacular volcanoes, and bubbling **geysers**. Its nearest neighbor is Australia, over 1,000 miles (1,600 kilometers) away. The two main population groups are the European **settlers** and the **Māori**. But people from **Polynesia**, Asia, and other parts of the world live there as well.

Cultural life

Māori myths and language dominate the country's culture, along with European sports, such as **cricket** and **rugby**. When a New Zealander greets you, you will either shake hands or perform a *hongi*. This is a meeting of foreheads and noses. *Hongi* means "one breath."

Welfare matters

New Zealand is a young, forward-thinking country of over four million people. It has had a **parliamentary democracy** for about 200 years. In 1893 it became one of the first countries to allow women to vote. The country was one of the first in the world to create laws for old-age **pensions**, minimum wages, and child health services.

How to say...

These words are in the Māori language.

Good morning	*Ata mārie*	(aahta mahree-eh)
How are you?	*Kei te pēhea koe?*	(kay teh peh-heh-ah kweh)
My name is…	*Ko ... ahau*	(kaw ... a-hoe)
I come from…	*Nō ... ahau*	(naw ... a-hoe)
Goodbye!	*Haere rā*	(hi-eh-reh rar)

Māori people call New Zealand *Aotearoa*, "Land of the Long White Cloud."

History: Becoming One Nation

The human history of New Zealand began around 1000 CE, when **Māori** arrived in canoes from other Pacific islands. They discovered a country with good land for growing crops, as well as lots of hunting and fishing. Different Māori **iwi** (tribes) settled across the two main islands of the country. The *iwi* in the South Island hunted a giant flightless bird, called the moa, for food.

Daily life

Each *iwi* had a chief who had special *moko* tattoos. When the chief died, his head was preserved. These heads are called *mokomokai*. Each *moko* is different and contains information about the person's rank, tribe, occupation, and adventures.

Tribal strength

Throughout the 1600s and 1700s, Māori defended their land against European explorers. During this time, Māori communities developed a strong culture. Each *iwi* built its own meeting house, called a *marae*. Only members of the *iwi* or invited guests could enter this space.

This image of a Māori chief who lived in the 1800s was painted by Charles Goldie. Goldie was a celebrated New Zealand portrait artist.

In 1642 a Dutch explorer named Abel Tasman was the first European to spot New Zealand. He named the country Nieuw Zeeland, which means "New Sealand." He returned to Europe and spread the news of the new country and the people who lived there.

CAPTAIN JAMES COOK (1728–1779)

Captain James Cook was a British explorer who sailed around New Zealand and made the first maps of its coastline. Lots of places in New Zealand are named after him, including Mount Cook and the Cook Strait.

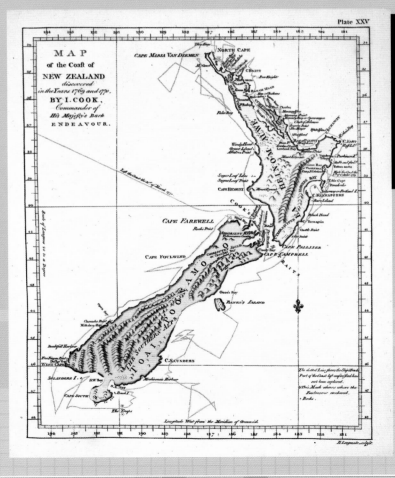

This is Captain Cook's map of New Zealand, drawn around 1770. It is very similar to modern maps today.

British rule

The Māori called themselves *Taangata Whenua* ("the People of the Land"). They considered all **Pākehā**, or non-Māori white people, intruders. The mainly British **settlers** established farms and towns. **Missionaries** built chapels and tried to convert Māori to Christianity.

A fair treaty?

By the 1830s, the British government wanted to make New Zealand a **colony**. On February 6, 1840, the **Treaty** of Waitangi was signed by the British and hundreds of Māori chiefs. The treaty gave Māori protection as British citizens, in exchange for rights over Māori land and fishing **resources**. Afterward, Māori tribes fought bitterly against the loss of their lands, but they were eventually defeated.

British officials and Māori chiefs sign the Treaty of Waitangi in 1840.

Daily life

In the 1860s, there was a major gold rush in the central South Island. Thousands traveled to New Zealand hoping to get rich. Each person bought an area of land where he or she could dig for gold. The camps were dirty and disease-ridden, and many people died there.

In 1841 New Zealand became a self-governing British colony. The town of Russell became the nation's first capital, and the new country's flag had a small **Union Jack** in the corner, to show its link with Great Britain. In 1893 women were given the vote—over 20 years before they could vote in Great Britain, and almost 30 years before they could vote in the United States.

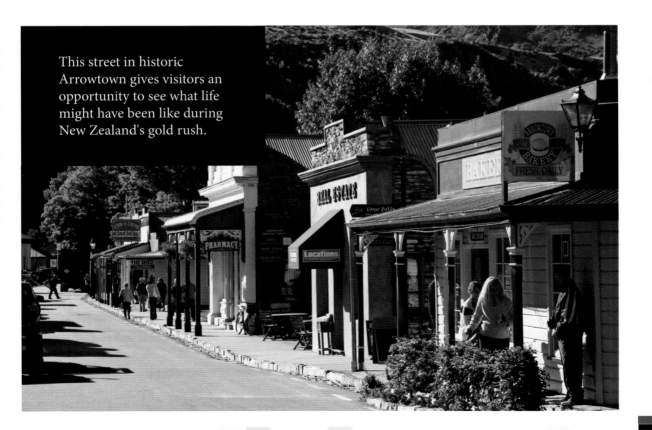

This street in historic Arrowtown gives visitors an opportunity to see what life might have been like during New Zealand's gold rush.

World at war

During the world wars, New Zealand soldiers fought alongside the British and Americans. During World War I (1914–18), over 100,000 young men sailed far from home to defend Britain from Germany. Over 3,000 Australian and New Zealand Army Corps ("Anzac") soldiers fought and died at Gallipoli, in Turkey. During World War II (1939–45), over 28,000 New Zealand soldiers were killed and more than 55,000 were injured. Today, the soldiers are remembered on Anzac Day, on April 25.

Modern state

In 1947 New Zealand became a fully independent country, but it remains part of the **Commonwealth**, and Britain's Queen Elizabeth II is **head of state**. The country has close ties with Australia, working together on defense, business, and shared workers. New Zealand also has a defense treaty with the United States, to ensure national security. Many people **emigrate** to New Zealand from all over the world for the quality of life it offers.

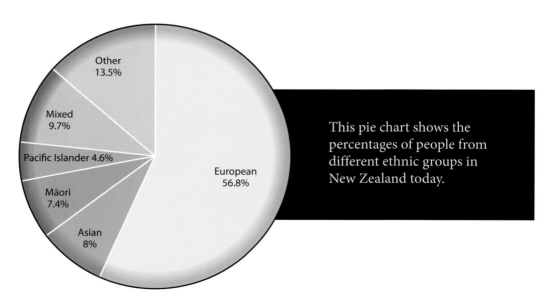

Other
13.5%

Mixed
9.7%

Pacific Islander 4.6%

Māori
7.4%

Asian
8%

European
56.8%

This pie chart shows the percentages of people from different ethnic groups in New Zealand today.

Challenges ahead

Today, New Zealanders face natural and political challenges. Volcanic eruptions and frequent earthquakes shake buildings and crack roads. In 2011 an earthquake near Christchurch, South Island, measured 6.3 on the **Richter scale**. Over 100 people died.

The Treaty of Waitangi remains New Zealand's most debated document. The Waitangi **Tribunal** hears Māori complaints and pays compensation for lost land and property. The tribunal works with the government to ensure that Māori land rights are protected in all future building developments.

Daily life

Most New Zealanders prepare for earthquakes or volcanic activity by storing extra canned food and bottled water. They also keep batteries, flashlights, stoves, and a radio handy in case of power outages.

Auckland is New Zealand's largest city.

Regions and Resources: Landscape and Living

New Zealand lies in the southern Pacific Ocean, and it is made up of the North and South Islands and a number of smaller islands. It has a total area of 103,363 square miles (267,710 square kilometers), making it slightly smaller than the state of Colorado. Mount Cook is the highest point, at 12,316 feet (3,754 meters). The **Māori** call it Aoraki, which means "cloud piercer."

Land of fire and ice

The country's spectacular landscape is the result of its location in the Pacific Ocean's **Ring of Fire**. The South Island has the dramatic Southern Alps, as well as **fjords**, **glaciers**, lakes, and coastal plains. The North Island has over 20 active volcanoes. Hot springs, **geysers**, and mud pools are also common, especially around the town of Rotorua, in the north-center of the island.

Weather report

New Zealand has a mainly **temperate** climate. However, there can be strong regional variations, where the weather can be either very hot or very cold. December, January, and February are the hottest months, while June, July, and August are the coldest. In winter, Auckland has more than 20 rainy days each month. In the summer, it gets an average of eight hours of sunlight per day.

How to say...

mountain	*maunga*	(mah-oonga)
river	*awa*	(ahwa)
sea	*moana*	(maw-ahna)
hot springs	*waiariki*	(wy-ah-ree-kee)
volcano	*puia*	(pooh-ee-ah)
coast	*takutai*	(tah-koo-tye)

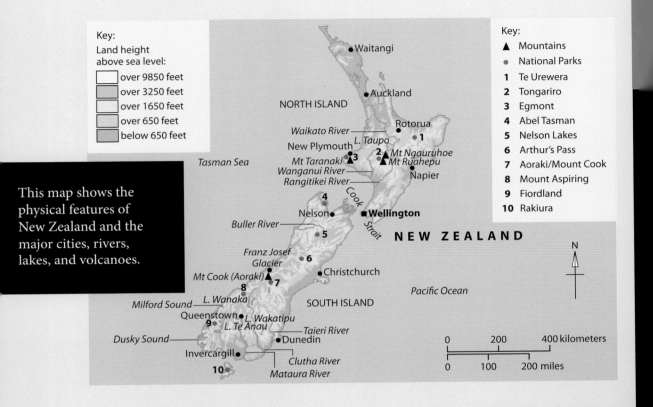

This map shows the physical features of New Zealand and the major cities, rivers, lakes, and volcanoes.

Key:
Land height above sea level:

- over 9850 feet
- over 3250 feet
- over 1650 feet
- over 650 feet
- below 650 feet

Key:
- ▲ Mountains
- • National Parks
- 1 Te Urewera
- 2 Tongariro
- 3 Egmont
- 4 Abel Tasman
- 5 Nelson Lakes
- 6 Arthur's Pass
- 7 Aoraki/Mount Cook
- 8 Mount Aspiring
- 9 Fiordland
- 10 Rakiura

Waitangi

Auckland

NORTH ISLAND

Rotorua

1

Waikato River

L. Taupo

New Plymouth

2 ▲ Mt Ngauruhoe

▲3

Mt Taranaki ▲ Mt Ruahepu

Tasman Sea

Wanganui River

Rangitikei River

Napier

4

Nelson

Cook

■ **Wellington**

Strait

Buller River

5

N E W Z E A L A N D

Franz Josef Glacier

6

Mt Cook (Aoraki) ▲

Christchurch

Pacific Ocean

8

7

Milford Sound

L. Wanaka

SOUTH ISLAND

Queenstown

9 L. Wakatipu

L. Te Anau

Taieri River

Dusky Sound

Dunedin

Invercargill

Clutha River

10

Mataura River

N

0   200   400 kilometers

0   100   200 miles

These are the bubbling hot springs of Whakarewarewa, near Rotorua, North Island.

New Zealand's regions

New Zealand is divided into 16 regions (see map on page 23). Canterbury, in the South Island, has the largest area, with 17,508 square miles (45,346 square kilometers). Auckland, in the North Island, has the highest population, at 1,462,000. More people live in Auckland than in the whole of the South Island. Of the total population of 4.2 million, 86 percent live in cities.

Farming focus

Agriculture is one of the most important industries in New Zealand. It employs over 110,000 people. Today, there are an estimated 40 million sheep in farms around the country. There are over 13,000 dairy farms producing over 3.4 billion gallons (13 billion liters) of milk every year. Over 8.8 million pounds (4 million kilograms) of butter and over 4.4 million pounds (2 million kilograms) of cheese are **exported** every year.

Dairy products such as milk, butter, and cheese are New Zealand's biggest exports.

YOUNG PEOPLE

Many young people travel around and to New Zealand to work on organic farms. They are not paid for working, but they get free food and board instead. These workers are called WWOOFERS, which stands for "Worldwide Opportunities on Organic Farms."

There are over 600 wineries in New Zealand.

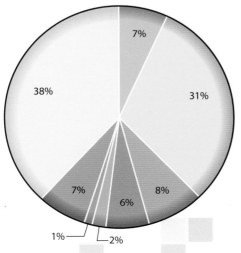

7%

38%

31%

7%

6%

8%

1%

2%

Key:
- dairy
- sheep
- beef
- other livestosck
- commercial gardening
- crops
- forestry
- not farmed

This pie chart shows the major land uses in New Zealand.

Business matters

New Zealand's **economy** is worth around $120 billion each year. Australia is its biggest trading partner, followed by the United States, China, Japan, and the United Kingdom. The currency is the New Zealand dollar (NZ$). New Zealand has a workforce of 2.3 million people, and the average yearly income is $27,400.

Manufacturing and tourism are major industries in New Zealand. The country also has a large food processing industry, as well as many wood and paper mills, **textile** factories, banking and insurance companies, and mines.

Natural resources and green expertise

New Zealand's best **natural resource** is its stunning landscape, which attracts 2.5 million visitors each year. Seventy-four percent of the country's workforce is involved in services such as tourism. The country also has supplies of natural gas, iron ore, sand, coal, timber, gold, and limestone. New Zealand's engineers are world leaders in using **hydroelectric** power.

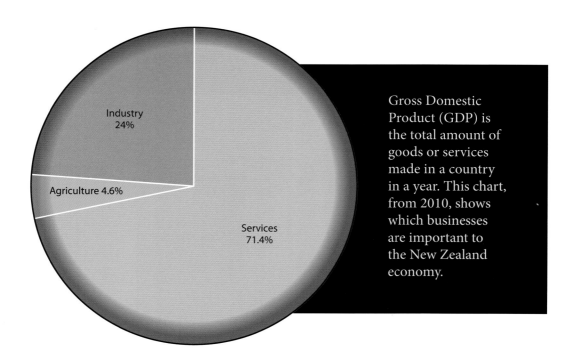

Industry
24%

Agriculture 4.6%

Services
71.4%

Gross Domestic Product (GDP) is the total amount of goods or services made in a country in a year. This chart, from 2010, shows which businesses are important to the New Zealand economy.

Ice climbing on the Franz Josef glacier is a popular tourist activity.

Daily life

The global financial problems that began in 2007 caused many job losses. However, New Zealand's unemployment rate of 6.4 percent is lower than many other well-off countries. Still, youth unemployment and **Māori** unemployment are big issues, with 16.2 percent of these groups out of work.

Wildlife: Protecting the Natural World

New Zealand is famous for birds such as the kiwi and kakapo. These birds have small wings and cannot fly. For thousands of years, they had no natural **predators** and did not need to fly away. When Europeans began arriving in New Zealand, they brought rats with them on their ships. Rats eat eggs and chicks, so many bird **species** are now threatened. The kakapo is so **endangered** that rat-free Codfish Island has become a kakapo **sanctuary**. It is estimated that there are only 120 still alive there.

Pest control

In 1837 the Australian possum was introduced to New Zealand. People hoped to trade its fur. Today, the possum is a pest that destroys crops and woodlands. There are an estimated 50 million possums across the country. The Department of Conservation puts down a poison called 1080 to try to control possums. Unfortunately, 1080 also kills some native birds.

The flightless kiwi is a national symbol of New Zealand.

YOUNG PEOPLE

The Kiwi Conservation Club (KCC) helps young New Zealanders learn about their environment. Over 16,000 members learn about native birds and wild places by going on adventures to local beaches and forests. KCC members also help on special projects, such as making nesting boxes for blue penguins.

The pohutakawa tree is known as the New Zealand Christmas tree because it blossoms in December.

Today, all visitors who enter New Zealand go through **biosecurity** to prevent any foreign seeds or creatures from entering the country. This is to protect the country's **unique** wildlife.

How to say...

animal	*kararehe*	(kah-rah-reh-heh)
whale	*parāoa*	(pah-raah-wa)
fish	*ika*	(ee-kah)
bird	*manu*	(mah-noo)
rat	*kiora*	(kee-aw-reh)

Managing nature

New Zealand is one of the most environmentally aware countries in the world. There are strict laws that ensure all new building developments are **sustainable** and that the country's **resources** are used wisely.

National parks

There are 14 national parks across the country. Two of these, Tongariro National Park and Te Wahipounamu, are on the United Nations' **World Heritage List** for their outstanding beauty and international importance.

Abel Tasman National Park is New Zealand's smallest national park. Its coast is dotted with white, sandy beaches and beautiful coves.

Daily life

The people of the Ngati Wahiao *iwi* have been using the **natural resources** of New Zealand for over 200 years. Their houses, stores, and school are built over hot springs and bubbling mud pools. They use the hot water for washing, heating, and cooking.

Over 25 percent of New Zealand is made up of forests. Plantation forests contain non-native pine trees, which are cut down and used for building. Native hardwoods such as the giant kauri are protected and can only be used if the tree falls naturally.

Eco-challenges

Air pollution, carbon dioxide emissions, and **ozone depletion** are three major challenges facing the country today. The national airline, Air New Zealand, is testing a new fuel called jatropha oil to power its airplanes. Jatropha oil is a **biofuel** and less harmful to the environment than jet fuel.

Non-nuclear

All New Zealand's energy is created from **hydroelectric** power, wind power, and power stations that run on gas or coal. There are no **nuclear** power stations in the country. Nuclear ships or submarines from other countries are banned from entering its waters or harbors.

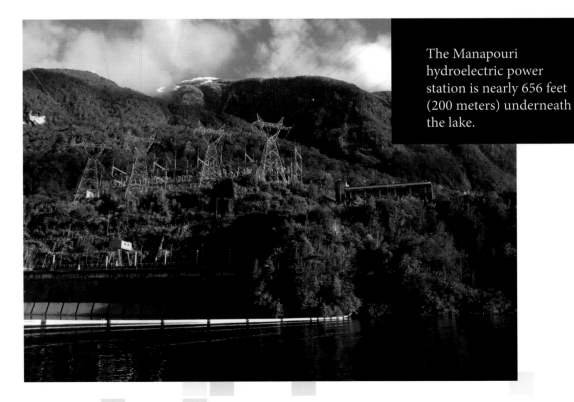

The Manapouri hydroelectric power station is nearly 656 feet (200 meters) underneath the lake.

Infrastructure: Politics and People

As part of the **Commonwealth**, New Zealand's **head of state** is Britain's Queen Elizabeth II. Her representative is the governor-general, who in turn represents New Zealand internationally. The **prime minister** is the head of the government. All official documents are written in English and in **Māori**, and the New Zealand government is also called *Kāwanatanga o Aotearoa*.

DAME JENNY SHIPLEY (BORN 1952)

In 1997 Dame Jenny Shipley became the first female prime minister of New Zealand. She served for two years before another woman was appointed to the post. Helen Clark (born 1950) was prime minister from 1999 to 2008.

House of Representatives

The New Zealand **parliament** is known as the House of Representatives, or *Pāremata Aotearoa*. It is usually made up of 120 members who represent different political parties. The members are voted in every three years. Anyone over the age of 18 can vote, and each voter has two votes. The first vote is to choose a local member of parliament. The second is to choose a political party. The party with the most votes gets the most seats in parliament.

The "Beehive" parliament building is in Wellington. It is built on special springs so that it can withstand earthquakes.

NORTHLAND●Whangarei

AUCKLAND
●Auckland

NORTH ISLAND

Tauranga
Hamilton● BAY OF
WAIKATO PLENTY GISBORNE

New Plymouth
●   Gisborne
TARANAKI   ●
                ●Napier
WANGANUI HAWKE'S BAY
          ●Palmerston North

TASMAN   WELLINGTON
Nelson●   ■Wellington
        ●Blenheim
       MARLBOROUGH

Greymouth●

WEST COAST
             ●Christchurch
CANTERBURY

SOUTH ISLAND

OTAGO
SOUTH LAND   ●Dunedin
      ●Invercargill

0   200   400 kilometers

0   100   200 miles

This map shows New Zealand's regions and regional cities.

Multicultural, multi-faith

Since the early days of European exploration and settlement, New Zealand has been **multicultural**. The dominant faith is Christianity, and there are small numbers of Hindus and Buddhists, too. There is a small Islamic population as well.

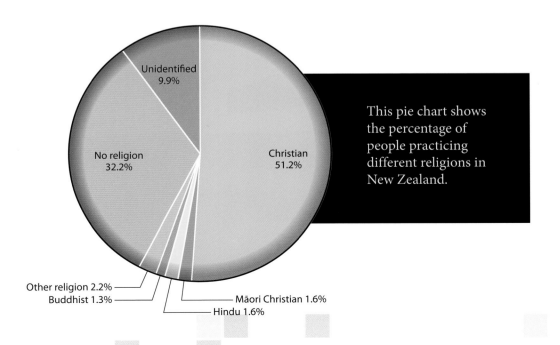

Unidentified 9.9%

No religion 32.2%

Christian 51.2%

Other religion 2.2%
Buddhist 1.3%
Māori Christian 1.6%
Hindu 1.6%

This pie chart shows the percentage of people practicing different religions in New Zealand.

Getting around

New Zealand has over 9,000 miles (15,000 kilometers) of coastline, 40 paved airports, 2,565 miles (4,128 kilometers) of railroad, and 58,353 miles (93,911 kilometers) of roads. New Zealand's mountainous terrain can be challenging for road builders and engineers. The Southern Alps have many tunnels and bridges built into them. In more remote parts of the North and South Islands, state highways are only one lane wide. The railroads are now mostly used by tourists.

Inter-island ferries transport people and vehicles between the islands around New Zealand. Water taxis are popular with commuters in the large coastal cities of Wellington and Auckland.

The TranzAlpine train travels between Christchurch and Greymouth, from one coast of New Zealand to the other.

Housing

New Zealand is a large country with a small population, so there is a lot of space. There are only 41 people per square mile (16 per square kilometer), and it is one of the least-densely populated of the world's wealthiest countries. Many houses are single-story dwellings, and most have a yard. Lots of New Zealand families also own a small beach house, called a "bach," that they use on weekends and during holidays.

Health matters

In New Zealand, every person is registered with a doctor. When someone is sick, they make an appointment to see the doctor and pay for the consultation. Usually, the government pays some of the cost of any medicine that is prescribed. If you are a visitor and hurt yourself doing an activity such as white water rafting, the government may pay some of your health costs, too.

This is a typical New Zealand detached house, built on its own land.

School life

New Zealand children begin school on their fifth birthday or the first school day after it. Education is free and **compulsory** until the age of 16. The school year begins in late January and finishes in mid-December. Students study a wide range of subjects, including English, math, science, art, sports, Māori, history, and **horticulture**. The United Nations' Education Index ranks New Zealand's education as first in the world, along with Denmark, Finland, and Australia.

Māori language schools

In the early 1980s, special Māori-language schools were opened so that Māori children could be taught about their culture in their own language. Today, approximately 10,000 children are enrolled in a *Kohanga Reo* (preschool) and a further 6,000 at a *Kura Kaupapa Māori* (elementary school).

At the age of 16, students can choose to continue on with school to study for a high school certificate. Alternatively, they can leave school to get a job, or study at a **vocational** school. Students go to college at 17 or 18 years of age. Of the eight universities across the country, the University of Otago is the oldest. It was founded in 1869.

How to say...

math	*pāngarau*	(pah-ngah-ra-oo)
sports	*tākaro*	(taah-kah-raw)
art	*toi*	(taw-ee)
music	*puoro*	(poo-aw-raw)
history	*tāhuhu*	(taah-hoo-hoo)
geography	*takotoranga papa*	(tah-kaw-taw-rahnga pahpah)
science	*pūtaiao*	(poo-ty-ah-or)

YOUNG PEOPLE

About 75 percent of homes in New Zealand have Internet access, and 91 percent of school children use it for their homework and social life. However, many Māori children do not have Internet access, although this number is slowly increasing with government grants. Facebook, instant messaging, and email are popular ways of communicating with friends.

School uniforms are common in New Zealand schools.

Culture: National Identities

New Zealand's diverse cultural life is a colorful mixture of **Māori** stories and beliefs and European art and sports.

Māori myth

Māori believe that a god called Maui discovered New Zealand. A myth describes how Maui went fishing in his canoe, which was the South Island. He dropped his magic fishhook over the side of the canoe and caught a huge, flat fish, which became the North Island.

Arts and crafts

A popular craft in New Zealand is woodturning. Native hardwood trees such as rimu and kauri are used to make beautiful plates, bowls, and furniture. Many Māori craftspeople make pendants out of greenstone or whalebone.

Māori shows include singing, dancing, and storytelling.

DAME KIRI TE KANAWA (BORN 1944)

Dame Kiri Te Kanawa is a celebrated opera singer. She was adopted by a Māori father and an Irish mother as a child and has recorded many Māori songs. She was awarded the Order of New Zealand, the country's highest honor, in 1995. Today, her foundation supports young New Zealand musicians.

Words and music

Janet Frame, Keri Hulme, Alan Duff, and Witi Ihimaera are well-known New Zealand writers. New Zealand musicians include Neil Finn, Dave Dobbyn, and Hayley Westenra. Westenra rose to fame for her classical singing when she was only 16. Jemaine Clement and Bret McKenzie are musical comedians. Their television show, *The Flight of the Conchords*, has a loyal following worldwide.

Brooke Fraser is a New Zealand folk-pop singer.

How to say...

The Māori way of doing things	*Tikanga Māori*	(Tik-ah-ngah Maah-aw-ree)
spear	*tao*	(tah-aw)
carving	*whakairi*	(fah-kah-ee-ree)
weaving	*raranga*	(rah-rah-ngah)
performing arts	*kapa haka*	(kah-pah hah-kah)
storytelling	*whaikorero*	(fah-ee-kaw-eh-raw)

Sports action

New Zealanders are passionate about sports. The country is world famous for adventure sports such as skydiving, whitewater rafting, and bungee jumping.

Don't look down!

Queenstown is New Zealand's adventure sports capital. In the 1980s, the first bungee jumping business opened there. In bungee jumping, a person's ankles are tied to an elastic rope. Then the person jumps off a high structure, like a bridge. The elastic stretches, and the jumper bounces up and down several times.

It is very important to have expert supervision if you want to try bungee jumping!

SIR EDMUND HILLARY (1919–2008)

Sir Edmund Hillary is New Zealand's most famous mountaineer. His image is on the country's five-dollar bill. In 1953 he and Tenzing Norgay from Nepal became the first people to climb Mount Everest, the world's highest mountain.

Leisure and sports

Rugby is New Zealand's national sport, and the All Blacks are the national team. New Zealand has many successful sports teams, including the Black Caps in **cricket**. Many people cycle, mountain bike, and take part in outdoor activities. When New Zealanders say they are "tramping," they mean they are going hiking. In the hills and mountains, there are huts where trampers can prepare food and sleep before continuing on the next day.

Each year many people take part in triathlons (contests that have three events) as well as in the Coast-to-Coast challenge. This takes place on the South Island and involves cycling, running, and kayaking.

The All Blacks perform the dramatic *haka*—a Māori war challenge or dance—before every rugby match they play.

A festival of food

New Zealand is one of the world's largest producers of kiwi fruit. Today, there are more than 32,000 acres (13,000 hectares) of kiwi fruit orchards around the country. Many towns in New Zealand hold food festivals to celebrate local produce.

The country's wines and beers are famous for their quality. New Zealand is one of the world's leading producers of Sauvignon Blanc wine. New Zealand lamb is celebrated for its sweet flavor. Seafood is also popular. Salmon, crayfish, oysters, and mussels are eaten along with *pipis* and *tuatua*, which are types of native shellfish.

A *hangi* is an earth oven that Māori and other New Zealanders use for cooking on special occasions. A pit is dug and hot stones are placed at the bottom. Baskets of food are put on top of the stones, and everything is covered with earth for several hours to let the food cook. The food is then passed around and shared.

How to say...

food	*kai*	(kye)
sugar	*huka*	(hooka)
milk	*miraka*	(mee-rah-ka)
oyster	*tuangi*	(too-ahngee)
apple	*āporo*	(aah-paw-raw)
bread	*pararoa*	(pah-rah-oar)
sweet potato	*kumara*	(koo-mah-ra)

Anzac cookies

Ask an adult to help you make these delicious treats. Anzac cookies were sent to soldiers fighting in World War II.

Ingredients

- 1 cup quick cooking oats
- 1 cup dried coconut
- 3/4 cup all-purpose flour
- 1/2 cup sugar
- 7 tablespoons butter
- 1 tablespoon maple syrup
- 1 teaspoon baking soda

What to do

1. Heat the oven to 350 °F (180 °C). Put the oats, coconut, flour, and sugar in a bowl.
2. Melt the butter in a small saucepan and stir in the syrup. Add the baking soda to 2 tablespoons of boiling water, then stir it into the pan.
3. Make a well in the middle of the dry ingredients and pour in the butter and golden syrup mixture. Mix together gently.
4. Put teaspoons of the mixture onto buttered baking sheets. Bake for 8–10 minutes, until golden.Put on a wire rack to cool.

New Zealand Today

Known the world over as a peaceful, environmentally responsible country, New Zealand today is a nation with a strong sense of **identity**. European and **Māori** cultures are trying to overcome the tensions of the past and live peacefully side-by-side. More Māori names for landmarks are being used instead of European names. Mount Cook is now usually called *Aoraki*.

Lights, camera, action!

The media industry is thriving in New Zealand, with film and animation companies working on major film productions. New Zealand director Peter Jackson won several Oscars for his *Lord of the Rings* movies, and New Zealand actor Russell Crowe won an Oscar for his role in *Gladiator*.

Green living

New Zealand is at the forefront of **sustainable** development and clean technologies. New Zealand has claims to territory in Antarctica, and the country has a permanent scientific base there. Scientists study climate change and assess the environmental impact of oil exploration.

The New Zealand film industry is helping to show the country's amazing landscape around the world.

The challenges ahead

The damage done to New Zealand's environment by introduced animal and plant **species** is a huge problem to overcome. Māori are often less wealthy than *Pākehā* and have fewer job opportunities. There are also still land claims to settle arising from the Waitangi **Treaty**. Youth unemployment is high, and many educated young New Zealanders leave the country to experience life overseas in Europe and the United States, causing a skills shortage at home. The country has suffered devastating natural disasters, such as the 2011 Christchurch earthquake. However, the people are united in their efforts to rebuild their communities and restore their way of life.

Today, New Zealand faces many of the same political and social challenges as other wealthy nations. No matter what the future brings, New Zealand is confidently making its global mark and finding peaceful solutions.

More than 140 people were killed and much of Christchurch was destroyed in the 2011 earthquake.

Fact File

Official languages: English, **Māori**

Population: 4,290,347 (July 2011 est.)

Area: 103,363 square miles (267,710 square kilometers)

Bordering countries: no land borders

Capital city: Wellington

Largest city (population): Auckland (1.36 million)

Main religions: Christianity, Hinduism, Buddhism

Life expectancy at birth: Men—78.4 years; women—82.4 years

World Health Organization ranking: 41st

Literacy rates: 99% of the population can read and write

Currency: NZ dollar (NZ$1 = US$0.75)

Gross domestic product (GDP): US$119.2 billion

Type of government: **Parliamentary democracy**; member of **Commonwealth**

Head of state: Queen Elizabeth II (represented by the governor-general)

Main political parties: ACT New Zealand; Green Party; Māori Party; National Party; New Zealand First Party; New Zealand Labor Party

National symbols: kiwi, silver fern

Climate:	**temperate** weather, with strong regional contrasts
World Heritage sites:	Te Wahipounamu, Tongariro National Park, New Zealand Sub-Antarctic Islands
Highest point:	Aoraki (Mount Cook), 12,316 feet (3,754 meters)
Major rivers:	Waikato, Whanganui, Clutha, Taieri, Rangitikei, Mataura, Manawatu
Flightless birds:	kiwi, kakapo, takahe
Natural hazards:	earthquakes, volcanic eruptions
Major volcanoes:	Ruapehu, Ngauruhoe, White Island, Rotorua, Taupo, Tongariro, Taranaki
Natural resources:	natural gas, iron ore, sand, coal, timber, **hydroelectric** power, gold, limestone
Major industries:	farming, wine, dairy products, tourism
Main imports:	machinery and equipment, vehicles and aircraft, petroleum, electronics, **textiles**, plastics
Main exports:	dairy products, meat, wood and wood products, fish, machinery
National holidays:	February 6 Waitangi Day April 25 Anzac Day June Queen's birthday October Labor Day

White Island is New Zealand's only active sea volcano. It churns out steam, ash, and sulfur.

Membership of international organizations: United Nations; World Health Organization; International Atomic Energy Agency; International Monetary Fund; APEC (Asia Pacific Economic Cooperation), South Pacific Forum

Other territories administered by New Zealand (dependencies): Cook Islands, Niue, Tokelau, Ross Dependency

Famous New Zealanders

Sir Apirana Ngata (Māori culture expert and politician); Georgina Te Heuheu (politician and first Māori women to gain a law degree); Ernest Rutherford (Nobel Prize winner for science); Jonah Lomu (**rugby** player); Russell Coutts (sailor); Sir Edmund Hillary (mountaineer); Bruce McLaren (race car driver); John Walker (athlete); Kiri Te Kanawa (opera singer); Neil Finn (musician); Hayley Westenra (singer); Michael King (writer); Witi Ihimaera (writer); Janet Frame (writer); Ngaio Marsh (writer); Charles Goldie (artist and designer); Peter Jackson (movie director); Sam Neill (actor); Russell Crowe (actor); Jane Campion (movie director)

National anthem

The most common national anthem for New Zealand is "God Defend New Zealand." This is usually sung in both languages—Māori first, then English.

E Ihowā Atua,
O ngā iwi mātou rā
Āta whakarangona;
Me aroha noa
Kia hua ko te pai;
Kia tau tō atawhai;
Manaakitia mai
Aotearoa

God of Nations at thy feet
In the bonds of love we meet
Hear our voices we entreat
God defend our free land
Guard Pacific's triple star
From the shafts of strife and war
Make our praises heard afar
God defend New Zealand.
—Juscelino Kubitschek (1902–1976)

Timeline

BCE means "before the common era." When this appears after a date, it refers to the number of years before the Christian religion began. BCE dates are always counted backward.

CE means "common era." When this appears after a date, it refers to the time after the Christian religion began.

about 1000 CE	Early settlement of New Zealand begins when **Māori** people arrive from other Pacific islands.
1400–1700	The Māori culture develops. Farming and hunting increase. Māori *iwi* are formed.
1642	Dutch explorer Abel Tasman sees the South Island and names it Nieuw Zeeland.
1769–70	English explorer Captain James Cook visits New Zealand.
1773	Cook's second expedition arrives on the South Island.
1777	Cook returns to New Zealand on board the *Resolution*. He maps the interior of the country.
1806	The first **Pākehā** (European) women arrive in New Zealand.
1814	Sheep, cattle, horses, and poultry are introduced.
1837	The possum is introduced from Australia and becomes a pest.
1840	February 6: Hone Heke is the first Māori chief to sign the **Treaty** of Waitangi. William Hobson becomes the first governor of New Zealand, and the country becomes a **colony** of Great Britain.
1840	Russell becomes the nation's first capital city.
1840s	The gradual settlement of New Zealand by Europeans takes place. Major towns and cities are established.
1854	**Parliament** meets for the first time. Māori outrage at the treaty results in war with the authorities. The Māori Wars last until the 1880s.

1859	Gold is discovered in Buller River, South Island.
1865	Wellington becomes the capital city and seat of government.
1867	Four Māori seats are established in parliament. All Māori men over 21 have the right to vote.
1869	New Zealand's first university is founded, the University of Otago.
1887	New Zealand's first national park, Tongariro National Park, opens.
1893	New Zealand becomes the first country in the world to give women the right to vote.
1914–1918	Over 100,000 troops leave New Zealand for Europe to fight in World War I. Many soldiers die at Gallipoli (1915) and Passchendaele (1917).
1940–1945	New Zealand soldiers fight overseas in World War II.
1947	New Zealand becomes independent and self-governing.
1953	Edmund Hillary and Tenzing Norgay are the first Westerners known to climb Mount Everest.
1975	The Waitangi **Tribunal** is established to settle land and **resource** disputes from 1840.
1987	The Māori Language Act makes Māori an official language.
1997	Dame Jenny Shipley becomes the first female **prime minister**.
2003	The population of New Zealand exceeds four million.
2008	Air New Zealand uses jatropha oil in a test flight.
2010	September 4: An earthquake measuring 7.0 on the **Richter scale** shakes the Canterbury Region, causing widespread damage but no deaths.
2011	February 22: An earthquake measuring 6.3 on the Richter scale shakes Christchurch, causing widespread damage and over 150 deaths.
2011	September–October: New Zealand hosts the **Rugby** World Cup.

Glossary

biofuel natural fuel that gives off less carbon dioxide than other fuels

biosecurity protecting a country's wildlife and nature from outside pests

colony country ruled by another country

Commonwealth countries that were previously a part of the British Empire

compulsory legal requirement to do something

cricket bat and ball game played on an oval field; it is similar to baseball

economy all the produce and trade of a country

emigrate move to another country to live and work

endangered when animals or plants are at serious risk of dying out

export sell goods to another country

fjord narrow arm of sea bordered by steep cliffs

geyser natural hot spring that squirts water and steam into the air

glacier slow-moving mass of ice

head of state person who is the chief representative of a country

horticulture study of plants and fruit

hydroelectric electricity produced by water power

identity set of characteristics that identifies a person or a culture

iwi Māori tribe

Māori Pacific Island people who were the first to discover New Zealand and settle there

missionary someone who goes to another country to work for a church and spread its faith

multicultural representing many different cultures

natural resource naturally occurring material that people can use

nuclear energy and power created by splitting atoms

ozone depletion thinning of the ozone layer, which makes Earth warmer and contributes to climate change

Pākehā non-Māori, white person

parliament ruling body of some countries; laws are made there

parliamentary democracy system of government in which citizens elect representatives, and these representatives, in turn, appoint high-level politicians such as the prime minister

pension government money given to people after they retire from work

Polynesia group of over 1,000 islands in the Pacific Ocean

predator meat-eating animal that hunts and eats other animals to survive

prime minister head of a parliamentary government

resource supply of a natural or artificial material used to produce goods

Richter scale system to rate the strength of an earthquake

Ring of Fire area in the Pacific where lots of earthquakes and volcanic eruptions occur

rugby game played with an oval ball that can be kicked, thrown, or passed

sanctuary protected area

settler someone who moves to a country and settles there

species type of animal, bird, or fish

sustainable using a resource so it is not permanently damaged or depleted

temperate neither very hot nor very cold

textile type of cloth or woven fabric

treaty formal agreement between two states

tribunal court

Union Jack flag of the United Kingdom

unique only one of its kind

vocational type of studies that prepare you for a particular job

World Heritage List list created by the United Nations of protected areas of outstanding natural beauty

Find Out More

Books

DiPiazza, Francesca. *New Zealand in Pictures* (*Visual Geography*). Minneapolis: Twenty-First Century, 2006.

Jackson, Barbara. *New Zealand* (*Countries of the World*). Washington, D.C.: National Geographic, 2008.

Smelt, Roselynn. *New Zealand* (*Cultures of the World*). New York: Marshall Cavendish Benchmark, 2010.

Strudwick, Leslie. *Maori* (*Indigenous People*). New York: Weigl, 2005.

Websites

www.kcc.org.nz

Learn about New Zealand's amazing wildlife and landscape through games and activities on this interactive website.

www.newzealand.com

Read about all sorts of topics related to New Zealand, from the food to the amazing adventure sports.

Places to visit

If you ever get the chance to visit New Zealand, these are some of the places you could visit and activities you could try:

Waitomo glow worm caves, North Island

Travel through a giant cave system by boat. See amazing rock formations guided by the light from millions of glow worms.

Buried Māori Village, Te Wairoa, Rotorua, North Island

The village of Te Wairoa was buried in the 1886 eruption of Mount Tarawera. Volcanic ash preserved many of the buildings, which means you can see how people lived over 100 years ago.

Harbor bridge climb, North Island

Climb Auckland's harbor bridge and get a bird's-eye view of the scenery.

Hot Water Beach, Coromandel, North Island

Grab a shovel and dig for your own hot water at this unique place.

Kaikoura Whale Watch, South Island

Take a boat trip to see whales, dolphins, and seals up close.

Punakaiki "pancake rocks," South Island

Walk around this amazing geological feature and see giant water spouts gush up into the sky through blowholes in the rocks.

Te papa Tongarewa, National Museum, Wellington

See some *mokomokai*, the preserved heads of Māori chiefs.

Waitangi National Trust (Treaty House)

Visit the place where the Waitangi Treaty was first signed in 1840.

Lakes District Museum, Arrowtown, South Island

Visit historic Arrowtown and see how the pioneers and early gold prospectors lived.

Topic Tools

You can use these topic tools for your school projects. Trace the map onto a sheet of paper, using the thick black outline to guide you.

The New Zealand flag has the **Union Jack** in the corner, to show its links with the United Kingdom. The red stars represent the four brightest stars in the Southern Cross constellation. Copy the flag design and then color in your picture. Make sure you use the right colors!

N

Wellington

Index